MW00958601

On my way across

The United States

BURK

Julie Schultz

I could not find Ohio,
And I failed my history test.
So I wrote this book
With all my heart
So you can be the best!

For my son, Parker:
The little boy
who says "shh"
when I sing.

ISBN-13: 978-1481807975

ISBN-10: 1481807978

© 2012 Dr. Julie C. Schultz
Associate Professor
of Education
Reinhardt University
Waleska, GA 30183

Dear Washington, D.C.:

I am learning all of my states. Please consider my application to become the nation's official bird.

Sincerely,

Burk the Turkey

When I got ready to go,
I *washed* my *orange car*...

on my way across
The United States.

WAsh=Washington

ORange= Oregon

CAr= California

On my *way*
up the *mountain*,
I thought *I'd never* get home!

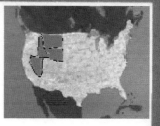

...on my way across
The United States.

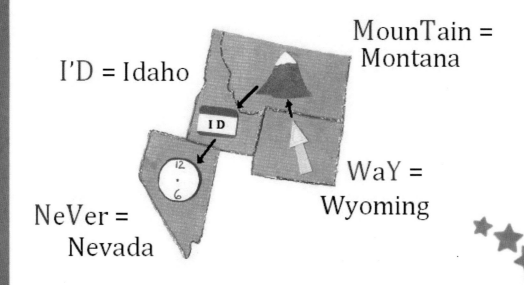

I'D = Idaho

MounTain =
Montana

WaY =
Wyoming

NeVer =
Nevada

I got so hungry,

I *cut a zillion new melons*...

on my way across

The United States.

CUT A Zillion New Melons...

UT = Utah

C° = Colorado

A Zillion =
Arizona

New Melons =
New
Mexico

Hey there's **Ned** and **Sid**--

new kids I met in tornado alley.

They said we'd be **okay** if we made it **Texas.**

..on my way across The United States.

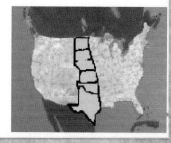

NeD=North Dakota

SiD= South Dakota

NEw= Nebraska

KidS=Kansas

OKay= Oklahoma

TeXas= Texas

I met a **man** named **Ian**. He had a **mohawk**,

And he walked **around** making us **laugh**.

...on my way across The United States.

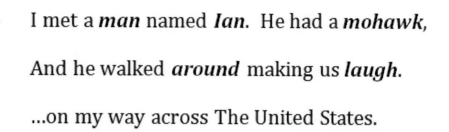

MaN=Minnesota

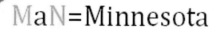

IAn= Iowa

MOhawk= Missouri

ARound=Arkansas

LAugh=Louisiana

Hey there's my new friend, *Will.*
He is a *minnow,*
and he always swims
down and around.

...on my way across The United States.

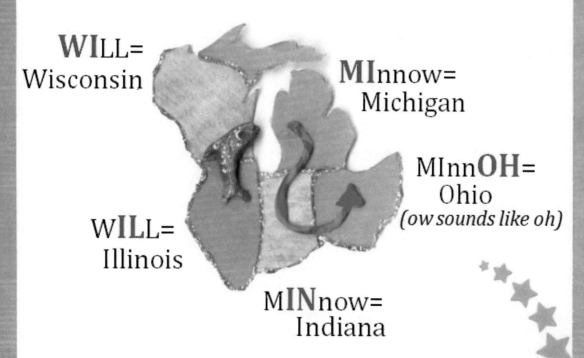

WILL=
Wisconsin

MInnow=
Michigan

MInn**OH**=
Ohio
(ow sounds like oh)

W**ILL**=
Illinois

M**IN**now=
Indiana

I went in search of the **key** to finding my **tune**.

I met **Ms. Alligator** at the hour of noon.

The **flowing** river, she pointed with care,

She said to follow and I'd find my heart's tune there.

...on my way across

The United States.

KeY=Kentucky

TuNe= Tennessee

MS.=
Mississippi

ALligator= Alabama

FLowing= Florida

Then I focused my *gaze*

and *scoured* the *north coast*,

as if expecting to see Blackbeard's ghost.

...on my way across

The United States.

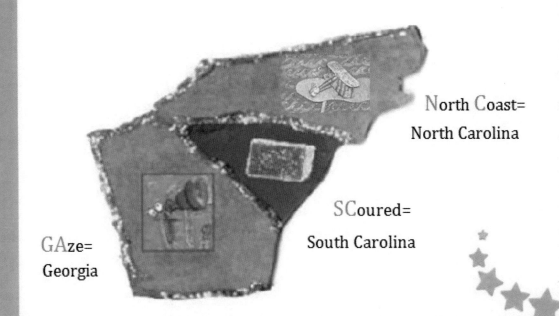

North Coast=
North Carolina

SCoured=
South Carolina

GAze=
Georgia

Next I *vacationed*
where three rivers flow.
Then I *waved* to my *parents;*
Only twelve states to go
...on my way across
The United States.

PArents=

Pennsylvania

WaVed=

West Virginia

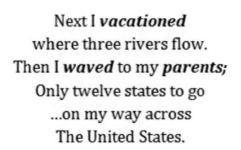

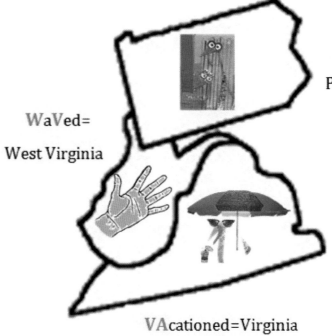

VAcationed=Virginia

I donned my *new jersey*
and *decided* that night
to cross the **Mason-Dixon,**
my *capital* was in sight

...on my way across
The United States.

New **J**ersey=
New Jersey

Mason-**D**ixon= Maryland

Capital=
District of
Columbia (D.C.)

DEcided= Delaware

I went over **Niagara yelling,**
the waters rushing so fast--
I can't believe my luck;
I **caught** a **ride** on a **mast**

...on my way across
The United States.

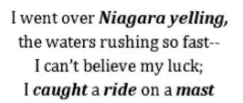

Niagara Yelling=
New York

MAst= Massachusetts

RIde= Rhode Island

CaughT=
Connecticut

When in search of a new place
for my very own
my *vote* I happily cast--
Tip Top, my **new home**
...on my way across The United States

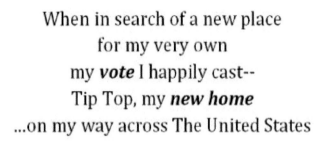

VoTe=Vermont

New Home=

New Hampshire

Now I've **met all** these **kids**

all over this land.

I've said **hi** to each all over this land.

I'm at my journey's end; what a trip it's been

...on my way across

The United States.

<u>A</u>ll <u>K</u>ids=
Alaska

<u>ME</u>t=
Maine

<u>HI</u>= Hawaii

Dear Burk the Turkey,

Great job! The minute I need an assistant, you will be the perfect bird for the job! You make birds everywhere proud to live in America!

Best Wishes,

Bald Eagle
Nation's Bird

Burk's Crazy Journey

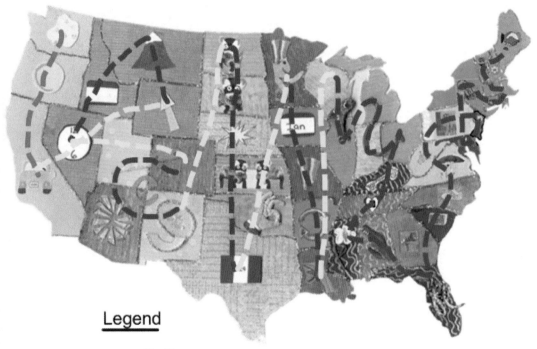

Legend

- - - ->   By Car

- - - ->   By Airplane

- - - ->   By Foot

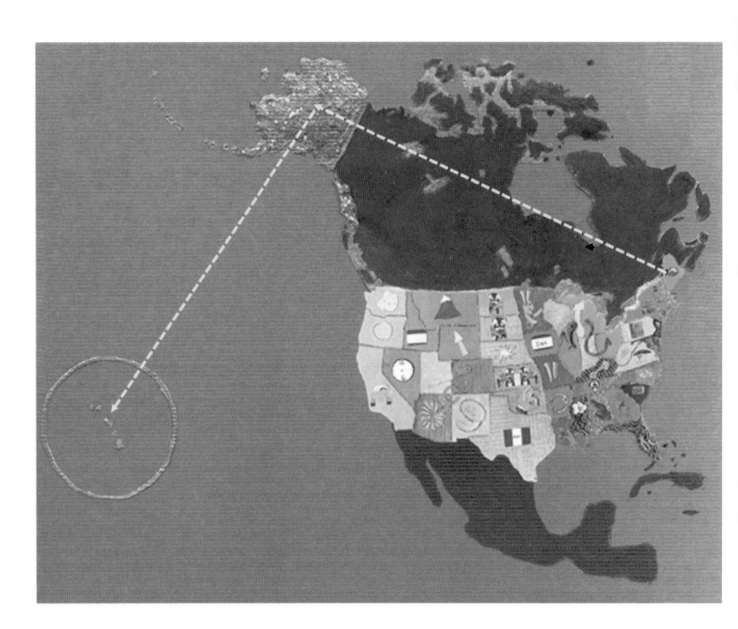

Also available to help you:

⭐ Song

⭐ Video

⭐ SmartBoard Interactive Lesson

www.teacherspayteachers.com/Store/Dr-Julie-Schultz

27574979R10021

Made in the USA
Lexington, KY
14 November 2013